Orca Origins

Rina Singh

DIWALI

Festival of Lights

ORCA BOOK PUBLISHERS

Library and Archives Canada Cataloguing in Publication

Singh, Rina, 1955–, author
Diwali: festival of lights / Rina Singh.
(Orca origins)

Includes index.

Issued in print and electronic formats.
ISBN 978-1-4598-1007-5 (bound).—ISBN 978-1-4598-1008-2 (pdf).—
ISBN 978-1-4598-1009-9 (epub)

1. Divali—Juvenile literature. I. Title.
BL1239.82.D58S56 2016   j294.5'36   C2016-900499-6
c2016-900500-3

First published in the United States, 2016
Library of Congress Control Number: 2016931882

Summary: Enlivened by personal stories, *Diwali* illuminates and celebrates how Hindu, Sikh and Jain traditions are kept alive in the modern world in this work of nonfiction for middle readers.

Orca Book Publishers gratefully acknowledges the support for its publishing programs provided by the following agencies: the Government of Canada through the Canada Book Fund and the Canada Council for the Arts, and the Province of British Columbia through the BC Arts Council and the Book Publishing Tax Credit.

Design by Rachel Page
Front cover photos by Getty Images, iStock.com, Dreamstime.com
Back cover photo by Amrita Singh

ORCA BOOK PUBLISHERS
www.orcabook.com

Printed and bound in China.

19 18 17 16 • 4 3 2 1

For Monique, who lights up my life

CONTENTS

Chapter Four:
Diwali Around the World

Marigolds.
Rina Singh

Lights of Diwali.
Rina Singh

INTRODUCTION

When I was a child growing up in India, **Diwali** was not only the most important festival and lasted the longest, but it was also my favorite. The word *Diwali* comes from the **Sanskrit** words *deepa*, meaning "light," and *vali*, meaning "row."

A row of lights. That's how I remember the festival—as an endless row of lights.

There was something magical about Diwali—the lights, the shopping, the sparklers, the fireworks and **mithai**, the sweets that gave me a sweet tooth. Schools closed down for ten days before Diwali and we felt the excitement in the air.

My favorite memory is watching my mom pour mustard oil into **diyas**, or oil lamps made of clay,

Looking at Diwali lights. I think my father totally captured my amazement.

B.S. Sodhi

and arrange cotton wicks in them. She then set them in large platters called **thaalis** that I eagerly carried to my father. I stood by his side as he lit the diyas and placed them around the house. After that I would stand back and let myself be dazzled by the lamps lighting up the darkest night of the month.

Then we all gathered in my mom's **puja**, or prayer, room to offer prayers to Lakshmi, the goddess of wealth. The room also had pictures of the Sikh **gurus**, or spiritual teachers. My mother is Hindu and my father is Sikh. Sikhs believe in one god, and Hindus worship millions of gods and goddesses. No one told me to pray to any god in particular. I just prayed because everyone around me did. It didn't occur to me to question if we were celebrating a Hindu Diwali or a Sikh Diwali. It was just Diwali.

My mother's prayer (puja) room with pictures of the goddess Lakshmi and Guru Nanak side by side on Diwali night.
M.S. Sodhi

Diwali lights.
Amrita Singh

Then I grew up, got married and moved to Canada in 1980. For many years after leaving India, Diwali lost its luster. Friends took turns hosting Diwali dinner and that was it. No lights, no sparklers, no prayers. Years passed.

One day, my daughter Amrita, who was in grade one at the time, came home and asked me, "Mom, what is Diwali?" Her question made me realize what I had left behind and what I could lose if I didn't make changes. Ever since that day I have celebrated Diwali with such devotion that even my non-Indian friends and their children have grown to love the festival.

So when the opportunity to write this book came my way, I felt the goddess Lakshmi was shining a light on me.

Diyas, or oil lamps, are put on small boats made of leaves and set afloat on the Ganges River in Varanasi.
SoumenNath/iStock.com

ONE

WHAT IS DIWALI?

The Hindu Legends of Diwali

Every year, in October or November, most Indians come together to celebrate Diwali. The dates vary from year to year as Diwali falls on the fifteenth day of the month of **Kartika** in the Hindu calendar. The calendar is based on the position of the sun and the moon. Diwali is celebrated on **amavasya**, the darkest night of the month. Originally a harvest celebration, Diwali has evolved into the biggest and the brightest of all Indian festivals. The several Hindu legends of Diwali celebrate the victory of good over evil and light over darkness. For Sikhs, Diwali marks the release of their sixth guru, Guru Hargobind, from prison. Jains celebrate Lord Mahavira's **nirvana**, or salvation from the cycle of life and death. No matter what the story, Diwali is a joyful holiday.

Buddhists also celebrate Diwali, because on this day in 256 BCE, Hindu emperor Ashoka gave up the path of violence and converted to **Buddhism**. He was instrumental in spreading Buddhism in India and abroad. The **Ashoka chakra**, a 24-spoke wheel representing the teachings of Buddha, is at the center of the Indian flag.

Rama, Sita and Lakshmana at the hermitage.
Wikipedia

RINA SINGH

Rama's Legend

On Diwali, people in North India celebrate the story of Rama.

In ancient times, Ravana, a mighty **asura**, or power-seeking deity, who had been granted powers over gods and demons by Lord Shiva, ruled Lanka (now known as Sri Lanka, a teardrop-shaped island at the southern tip of India). According to Hindu mythology, Ravana was a tyrant. His tyranny on Earth disturbed the gods, and they decided to send Lord Vishnu in the guise of a human to restore order.

And so, Rama, Vishnu's **avatar** (manifestation of a deity), was born to King Dashrath and his first wife in the city of Ayodhya. It was the custom for kings to have several wives. Dashrath's second wife bore him twin boys, Lakshmana and Shatrughana. Kaikeyi, his youngest and favorite wife, gave birth to a son named Bharat. She had once saved her husband's life, and he in turn had promised to grant her two wishes.

When Prince Rama came of age, he married Sita, a beautiful princess. When Dashrath decided to make Rama the king, everyone in the kingdom was delighted except Kaikeyi, who wanted her own son, Bharat, to be crowned. She demanded that Dashrath grant the two wishes he had promised her. She wanted Bharat to become king and Rama to be banished from the kingdom for fourteen years.

The heartbroken king had no choice but to keep his promise. Rama, without any hesitation, left with Sita, his new bride, and Lakshmana, his stepbrother.

In the forest, Rama, Sita and Lakshmana tried to make a life for themselves. One day, Sarup Nakha, Ravana's sister,

saw Rama and fell in love with him. When she wouldn't stop flirting with him, Lakshmana took out his sword and sliced off her nose. She turned into her demon form and rushed to Ravana and begged him to avenge the insult by capturing Sita.

The enraged Ravana set an elaborate trap to kidnap Sita. One day, when Rama and Lakshmana were away from their hut, Ravana snatched Sita and flew in his winged chariot to Lanka. A mythical bird named Jatayu tried to stop Ravana, but he slashed its wings. The distraught Sita dropped her jewels as a trail on the ground below, in the hope that Rama might find her. The dying Jatayu told Rama that Ravana had kidnapped Sita and taken her to Lanka.

Rama and Lakshmana set off for the island of Lanka and on their way encountered Hanuman, the monkey king.

Lakshmana, Rama and Sita.
Belyaev71/Dreamstime.com

Hanuman, who became a devotee of Rama, called his army of monkeys to make a bridge of boulders and tree trunks to Lanka. Together, they fought a fierce battle with Ravana and his army of demons. Every time Rama shot a crescent-shaped arrow to cut off Ravana's head, another head would grow in its place. This happened nine times. Rama then took out his last arrow, a gift from the gods, kissed it, and shot Ravana in the belly button, where he had supposedly hidden the nectar of immortality. Ravana fell to the ground, and Rama rescued Sita.

The fourteen years of exile were over. Twenty days later, they arrived in Ayodhya on the darkest night of the month. People of the kingdom had lit thousands of lamps to guide their beloved prince home. And so in North India, people light lamps to celebrate the homecoming of Lord Rama.

Krishna's Legend

Krishna and sacred cow.
santosha/iStock.com

In South India, people honor Krishna's story on Diwali.

In ancient times, a power-seeking deity named Narakasura became a worshipper of Brahma, the greatest of all gods. Pleased with Narakasura's devotion, Brahma told him that he could ask for any reward except immortality. Narakasura cleverly asked to have power over all males whether they were deities or humans.

Armed with Brahma's blessing, Narakasura began a reign of terror and ransacked every corner of Earth. He began looting the realms of the gods as well.

"Enough!" said the gods, and they went to Vishnu, the preserver of the world, to seek help defeating Narakasura.

At the same time, Vishnu was reincarnated as Lord Krishna on Earth, and he promised to help restore order to the world. Krishna asked his wife, Satyabhama, who was trained in warfare, to accompany him to battle Narakasura. It was the darkest night of the month and they summoned Garuda, a giant bird, and flew toward the enemy's fortress. Narakasura declared war by unleashing an army of demons on Krishna. Krishna slayed the demons and called on Narakasura to come and fight him face to face. Instead, Narakasura sent a thunderbolt, his signature weapon, and struck Krishna.

Satyabhama watched in horror as Krishna collapsed, and she furiously took out her own arrow and shot it at Narakasura's heart. For a moment Narakasura couldn't believe he had been struck because he thought Brahma's blessing had made him invincible. He soon realized that the fatal arrow came from the hands of a woman.

Woodern statue of Lord Krishna.
Muralinath/iStock.com

15

Lakshmi with elephants on the wall of the Hindu temple in Tirumala, India.
Shutterstock.com

"Life should be a continuous celebration, a festival of lights the whole year round. Only then can you grow up, can you blossom."

—Osho, Indian mystic, guru and spiritual teacher

Then Krishna arose, only pretending to have died, and walked with Satyabhama to the dying Narakasura. Narakasura apologized and admitted that he had misused his powers. He made Krishna and Satyabhama promise that the night of his death would be celebrated with lights and a lot of noise.

Upon his return, Krishna had a ceremonial bath with scented oils to cleanse himself of the bloodshed of the battlefield. And so in South India, before the prayers are said and lamps are lit, men bathe in scented oils. This reminds them of the battle that Krishna waged to rid the world of evil.

Lakshmi's Legend

Lakshmi, the goddess of wealth, is a central figure in the story of Diwali. She is often depicted with four hands, standing on a giant lotus flower, wearing a coral-colored **sari** and exquisite jewels. In two hands she holds lotus flowers, symbols of purity. Another hand is raised in blessing and the fourth hand holds gold coins, signifying her power to bring riches to those who pray to her.

Legend goes that there were ongoing battles between **devas** (gods) and asuras (demons). Indra, the warrior god, was responsible for the safety of devas. Lakshmi ensured that the gods remained prosperous.

Distressed by Indra's growing arrogance, Lakshmi left the realm of the gods and disappeared into the Milky Ocean. Without her, the gods became weaker and the demons began to assert their powers. Indra went to Vishnu for help. Vishnu told Indra that the Milky Ocean would have to be churned in order the get Lakshmi back.

After a thousand years of constant churning, the beautiful Lakshmi appeared, standing on a giant lotus flower. This happened on the fifteenth day of the month of Kartika in the Hindu calendar. It is the same date Diwali is celebrated every year.

The Days of Diwali

The beliefs are so varied and the gods so numerous that it would be impossible to say there is a single way to celebrate Diwali. This description of what happens during Diwali is a general one.

Dussehra (*dasha-hara* in Sanskrit) is celebrated twenty days before Diwali. It's the day Rama defeated Ravana,

Filled with gunpowder, explosives and firecrackers, the *effigy* of Ravana, the ten-headed demon king, is set ablaze in a spectacular show on Dussehra.
M.S.Sodhi

Firecracker-stuffed effigies of Ravana, his brother and his son are ready to be set ablaze on Dussehra.
M.S. Sodhi

Marigolds.
Dreamstime.com

the ten-headed demon. In the days leading up to Diwali, in most villages and cities in India, amateur actors perform the **Ramlila**, a theatrical rendition of Rama's life. The markets and bazaars get busier as people shop for new clothes, new utensils, firecrackers, diyas and of course lots of mithai.

On the first day of Diwali, also known as **Dhanteras**, people clean their homes and women shop for jewelry—from glass bangles to gold necklaces. A single diya is lit in the evening as an offering to Yama, the god of death.

Practices vary from region to region, but in many places the second day of Diwali marks Lord Krishna's victory over the demon Narakasura. People decorate their homes with marigold garlands and create intricate designs called **rangoli** on floors or in courtyards. Rangolis are usually made with rice flour and colored sand or powder. In South India, the designs are called *kolam*.

Gambling is considered good luck on Diwali.

The third day is the main day of Diwali and is celebrated by Sikhs and Jains as well.

The fourth day is the beginning of New Year, and the fifth day celebrates the bond between brothers and sisters. A sister performs a simple ceremony by putting a **tilak** (a mark made by mixing vermilion, water and rice), on her brother's forehead, and he in return gives her a gift and a promise to protect her.

Hindu Diwali

Lighting candles at the Golden Temple in Amritsar.
Rajesh Gupta

After the house is swept, the walls whitewashed and rangoli patterns made, it's time for Diwali to begin. Hindus in India wake up early and bathe, put on new clothes and do

Schoolgirls making rangoli—traditional designs made with rice flour and colored powders—to welcome the goddess Lakshmi.
Joginder Sharma

last-minute preparations for the evening celebrations. Boxes of mithai have to be distributed to family, friends and neighbors. Businesses in India close early so people can go home to their families. Women are busy preparing snacks, meals and sweets. In the evening, just as it's getting dark, families prepare for the Lakshmi puja, a ritual that welcomes the goddess into their homes. Diyas are set in steel or silver thaalis in preparation for **arti**, the ceremony of worship. The offerings also include flower petals, water, fruits and sweets. Saffron and vermilion are mixed with water and rice to make a paste so everyone gets a tilak on their forehead. The tilak is a symbol of the third eye of Lord Shiva. At the end of the prayers, everyone gets **prasad** (a portion of the food offerings), which indicates that the gods have accepted the prayers. Parents give their children money.

Mithai.
Rina Singh

People then light diyas around the house, especially on window ledges and along the entrance walls. Once the diyas are lit, families stay home to welcome the goddess Lakshmi, who is believed to visit homes that are brightly lit.

Then it's the time children look forward to—sparklers and firecrackers! The noise from the firecrackers reminds everyone of the battle that took place long ago. Some believe it lets the gods know that all is well with the world.

No particular dishes are served on Diwali. Every region in India has its own cuisine. The only common thing is that the meal is vegetarian and extremely rich, and there are sweets. Lots of sweets.

The night ends with watching the fireworks displays that many towns and cities organize. The next day, Hindus wake up to a new year.

"Regardless of the mythological explanation one prefers, what the festival of lights really stands for today is a reaffirmation of hope, a renewed commitment to friendship and goodwill, a religiously sanctioned celebration of the simple—and not so simple—joys of life."

—*Times of India* editorial

Guru Hargobind is released from Gwalior Fort by Jahangir's order.
Wikipedia

RINA SINGH

Sikh Diwali

From the time of Nanak (1469–1539), the first Sikh guru, Sikhs were strongly encouraged to celebrate the popular and seasonal festivals of India. When people congregated in large numbers, the gurus were able to spread their teachings, which gave new meaning to a festival usually celebrated by Hindus.

Sikh history unfolded during the Mughal period, which flourished in India from 1526 to 1707. The fifth guru, Guru Arjan, laid the foundation of the Golden Temple in Amritsar and compiled the ***Guru Granth Sahib***, the Sikh holy book. He added his own poetry to the poetry of all the gurus before him, and included compositions of Hindu and Muslim saints.

In 1606, Emperor Jahangir asked him to remove the compositions of Muslim saints. When the guru didn't comply, Emperor Jahangir sentenced him to death. He was made to sit on a burning metal sheet while hot sand was poured on him. After five days of inhuman torture, Guru Arjan was taken to a river for a bath, where he is said to have disappeared. Guru Arjan's martyrdom changed the course of Sikh history. The peace-loving Sikhs became fearless warriors in order to defend their faith.

Guru Hargobind, who succeeded his father, Arjan, as the sixth guru, wanted justice for his father's death. He strengthened his army and initiated his followers into martial arts. Because he felt threatened by Guru Hargobind's growing popularity, Jahangir imprisoned him in a fort where Jahangir had already locked up fifty-two other ***rajahs*** (princes) of independent kingdoms.

The Sikhs protested for more than a year, and on the advice of Mir Khan, an ally of the guru, the emperor agreed to free Guru Hargobind. But the guru insisted that the fifty-two princes be released as well. The emperor agreed on the condition that only those who could hold onto the guru's cloak would be allowed to leave.

Guru Hargobind asked his followers to make a large cloak and had fifty-two tassels attached to it—one for each prince. And so in 1619, Guru Hargobind walked out of the fort along with all the princes. He headed for Amritsar and arrived at the Golden Temple on the night of Diwali. The temple was lit to welcome Guru Hargobind just the way the kingdom of Ayodhya was lit to welcome Lord Rama.

And thus Diwali evolved with a Sikh identity and the event came to be known as *Bandi Chhor Diwas,* or the Day the Prisoners Were Freed.

The Golden Temple in Amritsar, the holiest of Sikh shrines, runs the largest community kitchen in the world! On a day like Diwali, more than 100,000 people eat langar— a free vegetarian meal offered to all regardless of their faith or social class.

The Golden Temple in Amritsar lit up for Diwali.
Dheeraj Paul

Carved detail, Mahavira Jain temple in Osian, India.
TerryJLawrence /iStock.com

On Sikh Diwali, pilgrims take a dip in the sacred tank around the Golden Temple early in the morning. They make offerings of money, grain, milk and other foods for the langar, the free vegetarian meal that thousands eat every day. At night, people float clay lamps in the tank and watch spectacular fireworks. Sikhs everywhere visit a **gurdwara**, or Sikh temple, light candles, sing hymns and celebrate with great enthusiasm.

Jain Diwali

Jains celebrate Diwali with great love and devotion. It's a historic coincidence that it was in the early hours of the Diwali morning in 527 BCE, when Mahavira, the twenty-fourth and last spiritual leader of the Jains, attained **moksha**, freedom from the cycle of rebirth. Jains light lamps on Diwali so they can keep the light of Lord Mahavira's knowledge alive.

Traditionally, Jain Diwali is a solemn celebration with fasting and keeping vows of silence. Orthodox Jains still celebrate it in a simple manner. However, socially, it was nearly impossible for most of the Jains to keep up with the austerity. Surrounded by so much festivity and noise, there was social pressure to join in with the Hindu celebrations. So Jains began to celebrate Diwali like the Hindus and many even do Lakshmi puja.

Saffron Coconut Burfi.
Rina Singh

> When making this recipe as well as the other recipes in this book, be sure an adult is around to supervise.

SAFFRON COCONUT BURFI

Ingredients:

15-20 saffron threads

4 tbsps hot water

2.5 cm (1 inch) cube of butter

2 cups desiccated (fine) coconut

250 ml (8 ½ oz) sweetened condensed milk

4 tbsps powdered milk

Directions:

Soak saffron threads in hot water and set aside. Melt butter in a saucepan and sauté coconut over medium heat for 3 to 4 minutes till it turns golden brown. Add sweetened condensed milk and stir constantly for about 4 minutes till the mixture loses its moisture and is reduced to a thick consistency. Add powdered milk. Strain and add saffron-colored water to the mixture, and pour into a greased shallow pan. Flatten the surface. Refrigerate for 1 hour and cut into squares. Serve cold.

Aditya's Story

Aditya sorting flower petals.
S. Bhalla

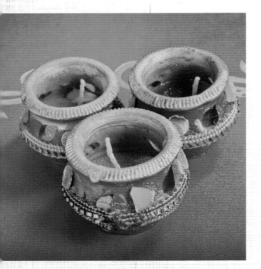

Diyas.
Amayra/iStock.com

Aditya Rattan is thirteen years old and lives in New Delhi. He shares his huge, sprawling house with his parents, his younger brother, his grandparents and a great aunt. He knows the rituals of Diwali well. He starts the day with a bath and wears new clothes. He knows the importance of cleaning the house, making a rangoli, and lighting diyas to direct the goddess Lakshmi to their home.

In the early evening, he visits his grandparents on his mother's side. His mother lights the first diya. Being the daughter of the family, she prays that Lakshmi will bless her parents' home. That makes Aditya's grandfather very emotional. Aditya and his brother receive gifts and they light a few firecrackers before heading home for their own family puja.

Aditya loves the way his house looks on Diwali night. "It glows and it feels as if stars have descended," he says.

His great aunt leads the prayers, and Aditya tries his very best to recite the *mantras*, or sacred chants, but since they are in Sanskrit, he finds it hard to keep up. Aditya's favorite deity is Lord Ganesha, the elephant god. "I don't believe in idol worship, but I think Lord Ganesha gives me strength. I prayed to him when I was being bullied at school. He gave me courage to face my bullies," he says with conviction.

His two favorite things to do on Diwali are shopping with his dad to buy firecrackers and then lighting them in the night, and eating ball-shaped sweets called **ladoos**.

He admits sheepishly that he knows firecrackers are dangerous and harmful to the environment, but he still loves them. "The loud sounds from the bursting of crackers scare Leo, my dog. Perhaps, Diwali is not for everyone," he muses. But more than anything else, Aditya loves the time he gets to spend with his family at Diwali. "It also makes me feel I'm part of something big and ancient," he says.

Celebrating Diwali in Pune, India.
Kuntal Saha/iStock.com

A group of North Pacific Lumber Co. workers in British Columbia.
Vancouver Public Library

TWO

THE HISTORY OF INDIAN IMMIGRATION

Coming to North America

United States

In the mid-nineteenth century, more than four million people came to the United States, but most of them were from England, Ireland and Germany. The Chinese Exclusion Act of 1882 prevented Chinese people from immigrating to the United States. An agreement with Japan in the early 1900s stopped all Japanese immigration. In 1917, a law against the immigration of people from Asia was added. Even when it was repealed in 1952, few people from Asia, including India, were allowed. It's not known how many people from India came before 1965 because they were listed as "Others" in the census records.

Gulab jamun, the most loved dessert of India, actually originated in Persia (now Iran). Persian invaders brought the recipe to India in the 13th century, where it was adopted and modified. The deep-fried dough balls are soaked in light sugary syrup and flavored with rose water.

Diwali Facts

India is the second-biggest producer of fireworks in the world. Sivakasi, a town in the state of Tamil Nadu, manufactures 90 percent of the fireworks for domestic consumption.

More than 700,00 people work in factories that have been described as open science labs using harmful chemicals like potassium nitrate and sulfur. The factories don't always observe proper safety standards, and most of the people in them work without masks and gloves. Sivakasi has been dubbed India's "Dangerous Fireworks Capital" because of frequent accidents.

Diwali fireworks.
Nikhil Gangavane / iStock.com

The 1960s brought changes to immigration laws because by then the United States was a prosperous country and was beginning to become involved in world affairs. The Immigration and Nationality Act of 1965 removed barriers for immigrants. Until then, the United States was not a preferred destination for immigrants from India. They mostly chose England or Canada. The new and more open immigration policy that was fully implemented in 1968 allowed the United States to bring educated and skilled newcomers from other countries. Scientists, doctors, engineers and teachers began to arrive from India. By 1980, there were more than 400,000 Indians living in the United States. Most of them spoke English, and they chose to blend in rather than stand out, as they were busy building their lives in a new land. There are believed to be 3.9 million people of Indian origin living in the United States today and 40,000 of them are doctors! Indo-Americans, as they refer to themselves, are among the most educated and richest people in the United States.

The first generation of Indian immigrants had to work hard to establish themselves in the new country—getting

legal status, buying homes and saving for their children's education. Some were too preoccupied to even maintain their religious traditions. It's only recently that Indo-Americans have started being more open about their celebrations. President Barack Obama celebrated Diwali for the first time at the White House in 2009, and Diwali came to Times Square in 2013.

Canada

Vancouver, BC, in 1906.
Vancouver Public Library

In 1897, hundreds of troops from across the British Empire were brought to London to celebrate Queen Victoria's Diamond Jubilee. Among them was the Sikh regiment from India. After the celebrations, the regiment returned to British India via Atlantic Canada. From Montreal, the troops boarded trains to Vancouver, where ships carried them back to India. The troops returned home and told stories of Canada's natural beauty and its riches.

At that time there was famine in many regions of India, especially Punjab. However, the British in India continued to export food to Britain. Leaving famine and pandemics (widespread diseases) behind, Indians left their land and came to Canada in search of a better life. The first immigrants from India to Canada were Sikhs who arrived in British Columbia around 1903. Most of the immigrants were from Punjab and were either farmers or former soldiers of the British army who had served in India and Hong Kong. In 1906, there was an influx of immigrants, mostly Sikhs, to the cities of Victoria and Vancouver. Although very few were Hindus or Muslims, Canadians

Vancouver, BC, in 1907.
Vancouver Public Library

Immigrants at the CPR pier in Vancouver loading possessions onto horse-drawn wagons.

Vancouver Public Library

In 2008, Google dedicated a Google Doodle to Diwali. The two o's were replaced by brightly colored bursting firecrackers.

called them all Hindus, and it became a ***racial slur***, a name used to insult anyone from the Indian subcontinent.

Chinese immigrants, mostly men who had been brought to Canada to complete the Canadian Pacific Railway, had already faced unimaginable hostility. Canada had imposed a "head tax" on the Chinese, and the tax went from $50 in 1885 to $500 in 1903. The Japanese, too, were viewed as "Orientals" and were attacked many times by racists in Vancouver.

Racial stereotypes prevailed, and anti-Asian sentiment was so rampant that when immigrants began coming from India, the country was alarmed and the Canadian press called it "The Hindu Invasion." Desperate to keep Canada white, politicians began looking at other commonwealth countries like Australia to help shape immigration policies.

In 1906, a new Immigration Act was passed, stating: *All immigrants must come to Canada by continuous journey from their country of birth or citizenship and have a through ticket purchased in their home country.* (Immigration officers were advised to use their own discretion for British and European immigrants.) It was impossible to have a journey without a stopover because there was no direct steamship line from India. The act also stated: *All immigrants from Asia must have in their possession $200.* (Immigrants from Britain and northern Europe were expected to have twenty-five dollars upon arrival.) Two hundred dollars was not only beyond most people's means, but also an inconceivable amount for Indians coming from India.

In 1907, another law was passed: no Chinese, Japanese or Indian was allowed to vote. All immigrants from Asia were stripped of their citizenship status as well.

Canadian Pacific was forced to shut down all steamship travel to and from India and was given a warning for selling one-way tickets to Indians. As a result, immigration from South Asia stopped for a few years, but that did nothing to improve the lives of Indians already living in Canada.

In fact, Canadians began to look for ways to get rid of Indians who had already settled in Canada. In 1908, Canadian officials met with the leaders of the Indian community and proposed that immigrants accept **indentured labor** in the West Indies. Indentured labor was a system of bonded labor that recruited people to work on cotton and sugar plantations for a period of three to five years. It was a new type of slavery, which had been abolished in 1834 throughout the British colonies. The rationale offered was that the tropical climate would be better suited to Indians. Two leaders of the Indian community traveled to British Honduras

A swastika made with flowers.
Nikhil Gangavane/iStock.com

The most sacred Hindu symbol, the swastika, was stolen and misused by the Nazis in the 1930s.

33

Clay diyas made by potters in Bangalore.
Hema Narayanan/Shutterstock

(now Belize) with Canadian officials to explore the possibility. The Canadians were hopeful that at least a thousand immigrants would relocate. Upon their return, the Indian leaders declared in a public meeting that they had been offered a bribe to paint a favorable picture for the community. That brought the entire scheme to an abrupt end.

On October 13, 1913, thirty-nine Sikhs arrived in Victoria via Hong Kong. They were detained, and H.H. Stevens, a Vancouver Member of Parliament at the time, unleashed his personal hatred toward them. "I challenge any man living to bring out a single instance in the whole history of the Indian nation to show that their civilization has done anything at all to uplift the other races of the world." Today it is almost unthinkable that anyone would express his or her hatred so openly. Stevens did everything in his power to stop the thirty-nine men from staying in Canada.

The Indian community hired a fearless lawyer named Edward Bird to fight the case. Bird argued that the men had come directly from Hong Kong, which was as much a part of the British Empire as India was. Chief Justice Gordon Hunter agreed with Bird's interpretation of the Immigration Act and allowed the men to stay. It was a victory that made headlines in Asia, where people were eager to migrate to Canada.

The *Komagata Maru*

Meanwhile, in Hong Kong, Gurdit Singh, a wealthy Sikh merchant, was unhappy with what was happening to South Asians in Canada. He wanted to test the changing immigration policies of Canada, especially after the Hunter decision. He chartered a Japanese ship called the *Komagata Maru*, and convinced 165 passengers to take the uncertain journey with him. In Shanghai, 111 Sikh passengers joined the ship; in Japan, 86 came aboard in Moji and 14 in Yokohama. Technically all passengers aboard were British subjects and could choose to live anywhere in the British Empire. They even had voting rights. There were 340 Sikhs, 24 Muslims and 12 Hindus. Reporters were tracking the journey at every port, so Vancouver was ready to do everything in its power to stop the Indians from setting foot on Canadian soil. When the *Komagata Maru* arrived, the passengers were dressed in their best clothes, ready to start their new lives. The authorities refused permission for the ship to enter the harbor, saying it had not come directly from India. Except for Gurdit Singh, no one had two

"Our physical alienation from India almost inevitably means that we will not be capable of reclaiming precisely the thing that was lost; that we will, in short, create fictions, not actual cities or villages, but invisible ones, imaginary homelands, Indias of the mind."

—Salman Rushdie, *Imaginary Homelands*

Aboard the *Komagata Maru*.
Vancouver Public Library

Crowded deck of *Komagata Maru*.
Vancouver Public Library

hundred dollars in his or her possession. Legally, Gurdit Singh, being a businessman, should have been allowed to disembark, but he was seen as a troublemaker and therefore denied entry into Canada.

The ship was kept three kilometers (two miles) away from the harbor, and only the Japanese crew was allowed to come and go. The passengers were told repeatedly to turn around and go back, but they refused. As a punishment, and to make them go back of their own will, only minimal supplies of food and water were sent to the passengers. The situation on the ship worsened. Starvation and unsanitary conditions made the passengers restless, rebellious and ill.

In the end, food and water were loaded onto the ship; then the Royal Canadian Navy arrived and aimed its guns at the *Komagata Maru* and forced it to leave. The ship had stayed in Canadian waters for two months.

On September 26, 1914, the *Komagata Maru* arrived in Calcutta to another hostile welcome. The British wanted all the passengers to be put on one train to Punjab, but when that met with resistance, the British opened fire and killed twenty people. The surviving passengers made sure Gurdit Singh was safe so he could tell the story of the unfortunate journey. "From start to finish, it's a sad story, but it is the story of my life," Gurdit Singh wrote in his memoir many years later.

In 2016, Prime Minister Justin Trudeau apologized in the House of Commons for the *Komagata Maru* incident. A century after the events, Canada Post commemorated the incident by issuing a stamp.

After the *Komagata Maru* Incident

Tensions between the Sikh community and the Canadian government escalated. After the *Komagata Maru* incident, Sikhs were sad and disillusioned. Some left for India to help overthrow the British rule. Families of those who remained in British Columbia were allowed to come in the 1920s. Sikhs worked hard to fit into Canadian society—many cut off their children's hair (the Sikh religion forbids the cutting of hair), and some made Sikh women wear dresses (rather than the traditional *salwar kameez*) in public. Sikh leaders inspected homes of their people to ensure high standards of cleanliness.

Inside Sikh temples, however, traditional Sikh culture was maintained. The temple leaders not only handled births,

Diwali Facts

Portuguese colonists brought marigold (*genda*) flowers to India in the 16th century. Marigolds are widely grown, and it's difficult to imagine any festive occasion, especially Diwali, Dussehra and weddings, without them.

Synonymous with celebration, marigolds come in all the favorite colors of India—yellow, gold, orange and red. They are sturdy enough to be threaded into garlands, and are affordable and unbelievably abundant. Symbolic of peace and prosperity, marigolds adorn doorways, porches, altars, temples and wedding pavilions in India.

Marigold garlands.
Rina Singh

Vikram's Everyday Chana Masala
Rina Singh

weddings, deaths and religious celebrations, but all problems related to health, employment and racism as well. The temple was truly the heart of their community. This is where religious celebrations were held in a quiet manner. The Sikh community was determined not to give the white Canadians an opportunity to criticize them for being different or bringing strange customs with them from India. Diwali was not a preferred celebration for Sikhs in those dark times when they were fighting for their very survival. Nevertheless, they celebrated the birthdays of the gurus. It was only in the 1970s, when there was an influx of immigrants from India and former British colonies,

Recipe by Vikram Vij

EVERYDAY CHANA MASALA

Ingredients:

½ cup canola oil

1 tbsp cumin seeds

1 ½ cups finely chopped onions (1 large)

1 ½ cups tomatoes chopped (2 medium)

1 ½ tsps salt

5 tbsps finely chopped ginger

4 tbsps finely chopped jalapeño peppers

3 cans (each 450 to 475 ml, or 15 to 16 oz) chickpeas, drained

1 cup coconut milk, stirred

8 stalks green onions, green parts only, chopped in ¼ inch pieces

Naan bread

Serves 6

Directions:

Heat oil in a medium pot on medium-high heat for 1 minute. Add cumin seeds and allow to sizzle for about 30 seconds. Add onions and sauté 8 to 10 minutes, or until they are brown. Stir in tomatoes, salt, ginger and jalapeño peppers, and stir well. Sauté for about 5 to 8 minutes, or until oil glistens on top. Stir in chickpeas and coconut milk. Bring to a boil, reduce the heat to medium-low, cover and simmer for 5 to 8 minutes. Stir chickpeas at least once while they are simmering. Add green onions, stir and simmer chickpeas for just 1 minute more, and then turn off the heat. Serve with naan bread.

that Diwali became a more visible celebration in Canada. Today, Diwali is proudly celebrated in all Hindu and Sikh temples across Canada.

The Continuous Journey law remained in effect until 1947. That was the year India gained independence from British rule. In 1966, the government of Prime Minister Lester B. Pearson introduced a more open policy, because there was no way for Canada to grow without immigrants. The immigrants who arrived from India in the 1960s were well educated—teachers, engineers and doctors.

In 1972, when Ugandan president Idi Amin expelled tens of thousands of Indians, the government of Prime Minister Pierre Trudeau agreed to take in three thousand people. Canada handled the situation with compassion and, in the end, six thousand political refugees of Indian origin settled here. Sadly, prejudice was still evident, leading directly to the "Paki-bashing" of the 1970s, in which gangs would commit violent attacks against South Asian immigrants, who were often referred to as *Pakis* (residents of Pakistan), even when they came from other countries.

In 2013, India, along with China, was the top source of immigrants to Canada.

Exterior of a Vancouver Sikh temple.
Vancouver Public Library

"When I was growing up in Rhode Island in the 1970s, I felt neither Indian nor American. Like many immigrant offspring I felt intense pressure to be two things, loyal to the old world and fluent in the new, approved of on either side of the hyphen."

—Jhumpa Lahiri, *Newsweek*, 1999

Swati's Story

Making Diwali crafts in school.
Courtesy of Swati Khurana

Swati Khurana is a New York–based writer, blogger and artist. She was two years old in 1977 when she emigrated from India with her family to New York.

As a kid, she desperately sought to fit in with "White America," but her skin color, culture and religion made it difficult. She recalls a kindergarten incident that sent her home sobbing. The kids called her a "bad girl" because Santa didn't bring her any presents. She says that a belated Christmas arrived that weekend, the first of her Hindu family's annual secular celebrations. There were times when she introduced herself to new people as "Sarah" instead of the less common "Swati."

As she was growing up, she continued to have many questions about her identity and culture. She remembers making Christmas cards and presents for her teachers and trying to find out about her friends' cultural traditions. But no one was curious enough to reciprocate and ask her about celebrations like Diwali.

Her memories of Diwali are simple. It was celebrated on the nearest weekend with a potluck dinner at someone's home. "We celebrated Diwali invisibly," she says.

It wasn't until college, in New York City, that she started to feel like herself. She reclaimed the identity that she had shunned in childhood.

Swati asked her daughter Shalini's teachers if the children in her class could do a Diwali project. She snipped colored file folders into the traditional shape of diyas complete with paper flames.

The following year, her daughter took the matter into her own hands and announced to her mother that they would be celebrating Diwali in her school with an art project. There would be saris for her friends to play with, *bindi* stickers (a bindi is a decorative dot worn in the middle of the forehead) to try on, and then they would read her favorite picture book—*Mama's Saris*. In the book, a young girl who is turning seven goes through her mother's saris in a suitcase, remembering the different occasions when she wore them.

Swati says her daughter's school celebrates Christmas, Hanukkah, Kwanzaa, Eid and Diwali. "To me, it sounds like an America where there is room for all of us," she says. Her blog entry on Diwali was published in the *New York Times* with the headline: "Diwali, Once Hidden, Now Lit Large."

In 1941, there were about 1,400 people of East Indian origin living in Canada, and according to the 2011 National Household Survey, there were more than a million.

Saris.
Abenaa /iStock.com

Nimrat's Story

Gurdit Singh shown in the cream suit.
Vancouver Public Library

Nimrat was six years old when she immigrated to Canada with her family in 2003. At the age of 12, she went on a family trip to British Columbia. Her family visited the *Komagata Maru* memorial, and it was there they told her that she was related to Gurdit Singh. Despite the fact that her ancestor was turned away from the shores of Canada in a hateful manner, her family decided to make this country their home. "Canada had evolved and become multicultural," she says about the family's decision to move here.

In 2014, her ninth grade English teacher put up a poster of the stamp that was issued on the one hundredth anniversary of the *Komagata Maru* incident. After the teacher discussed the historic event, Nimrat shared with her class that Gurdit Singh was her great-great-grandfather. That day, it dawned on her that she, too, was a small part of Canadian history. Nimrat remains in touch with her heritage by staying connected to her family in India through social media, taking Punjabi classes and celebrating festivals like Diwali.

Even though her memories of Diwali in India are fading, she clearly remembers there were a lot more firecrackers and fireworks there. In Canada, she goes to school on Diwali since the celebrations take place in the evening. After an early evening trip to the Sikh temple, where she

Nimrat posing with limited edition
print of *Komagata Maru* stamp.
Amrita Singh

Diwali fireworks in India.
Thefinalmiracle/iStock.com

lights candles, she goes to the street party that her mostly South Asian neighborhood in Brampton, Ontario, organizes. The neighbors pitch in to cook a feast in someone's garage. She loves the fact that most of her childhood friends live on her street. The evening ends with sparklers and firecrackers. She definitely wants to keep the tradition of Diwali alive as she steps into adulthood but is not sure if it will be the same in future years. But for now she is happy and feels safe, surrounded by her family, her friends and a great community. She has never experienced racism personally. That shows how far Canada has come as a society in a hundred years.

Children in India with sparklers on Diwali.
Nikhil Gangavane/Dreamstime.com

Lighting lamps for Diwali festival in India.
Thefinalmiracle/Dreamstime.com

THREE

THE EVOLUTION OF DIWALI

The Changing Face of Diwali in India

Some people in India say that Diwali is not what it used to be. They are concerned that the original traditions of Diwali are being lost, that the rituals have been pushed into the background and consumerism has taken over. In cities, Diwali has definitely become noisier and more commercial. In villages, however, it continues to be a simple festival, a harvest celebration after many months of hard work. The focus of Diwali outside the cities is on prayers offered to the goddess Lakshmi for cattle, grain and money, followed by wholesome feasts.

In cities like Mumbai, *Teen Patti*, a ceremonial three-card game usually played at home, has morphed into Blackjack and Poker at serious gambling parties.

India's sweet tooth could be blamed on the fact that India is the second-largest producer of sugar in the world. Indians consume 58 grams of sugar per capita per day, more than double the amount recommended by the World Health Organization.

47

Gone are the days of the beloved rockets launched from empty soda bottles. The firecrackers and fireworks today are louder, more elaborate and very sophisticated.

Diwali baskets filled with chocolates, nuts and cookies have replaced humble calendars with colorful pictures of Hindu gods and goddesses as corporate gifts.

The clay diya is still used for prayer ceremonies, and it is unlikely that this symbol of Diwali will ever go out of style, but scented candles and Christmas-type lights are commonly used to light homes.

Hallmark and local companies have started making greeting cards for the occasion—something unheard of even two decades ago.

Gift exchanges are the norm, and Diwali shopping has reached a new high. Small amounts of gift money given

Saffron is not only the most expensive spice in the world, but it is also considered the most sacred in India. Saffron is used in many recipes and religious rituals.

Meena Bazaar Market in Delhi.
Meinzahn/iStock.com

to children have given way for expensive wrapped gifts. Before Diwali, the sale of saris, electronics and toys goes up and so does the sale of washing machines and refrigerators. It is a time of renewal, after all. And merchants take full advantage of that.

In the past few years there has been a surge in tourist destinations like Goa offering Diwali holiday packages. Busy families are choosing to break the tradition of staying home for Diwali in order to better use their holiday time.

But at the same time, companies like PepsiCo have encouraged people to spend Diwali at home. The company's emotional 2014 ad campaign—*Ghar wali Diwali* (Diwali at Home)—struck a chord with younger people who work away from home. Many felt compelled to travel to their families to celebrate the festival of lights.

Fireworks.
Thefinalmiracle/Dreamstime.com

Mithai Gets a Makeover

In keeping with the changing culture of urban India, mithai got a makeover in 2014. American franchises like Dunkin' Donuts and Häagen-Dazs in New Delhi created Westernized versions of mithai. They started with mango-glazed donuts a month before, and by Diwali they had introduced *motichoor* ladoo and a gulab jamun donut. Both ladoos and gulab jamuns are popular ball-shaped sweets in India. One of the best-selling items was called "It's a Mistake," a white chocolate donut topped with guava and chili. Sales were huge and *The Wall Street Journal* picked up the success story. Reactions in the Indian community, however, were mixed. Diehard mithai fans preferred to stick to the traditional sweets,

Ladoo donut with silver leaf.
Rina Singh

Diwali Facts

In the past few years, Diwali has started to look as if it is "Made in China." From firecrackers to diyas, Chinese goods have exploded on the Indian market. Illegally imported from China, the firecrackers are cheaper, brighter and louder than their Indian counterparts. They are also more dangerous.

The simple clay diyas are also being replaced by plastic and wax versions. Cheaper and more convenient to light than clay diyas, unfortunately, the new versions are putting entire communities of potters out of business. The successful "Make in India" campaign, launched in 2015, is helping some Indians rethink their choices.

Vrindavan, India
Miragik/Dreamstime.com

but younger people loved the fusion. At 65 Indian rupees (about $1.30 Canadian) each, the new sweets sold out in Delhi by the weekend before Diwali.

Choko-la, a company in India, launched firecracker-shaped chocolates packaged in retro-style boxes, inspired by the boxes of firecrackers sold on the streets. It was a way to celebrate Diwali without really lighting firecrackers. There is a movement on the rise to boycott the use of fire-crackers because of child labor involved in the industry.

Widows Celebrate Diwali

An estimated six thousand widows live in Vrindavan, a small town in North India crammed with temples. According to the great epic narrative *Mahabharata*, Lord Krishna was born here and enjoyed the legendary love affair with his sweetheart, Radha. In the romantic town of Vrindavan, instead of *namaste* all greetings and conversations begin with *Radhe Radhe*, the name of Krishna's lover.

However, the town also has a dark side and is known as the "city of widows." It's a mystery why widows were first drawn to this town, but they all have sad stories to tell. They have been cast out by a society that believes widows are unlucky. Their own children, who want a shortcut to their inheritance, have driven them out of their homes. The families of widows pretend to bring them here for a pilgrimage and then dump them, or the women travel to this temple town on their own to live out the rest of their lives. Unwelcome at weddings and forgotten during festivals, these widows did something remarkable in October 2014.

Indian widows participate in Diwali on the banks of the River Yamuna in the northern city of Vrindavan on October 21, 2014.
Roberto Schmidt/AFP/Getty Images

A thousand widows, supported by nongovernmental organizations like Sulabh International, defied age-old traditions and took to the streets on the evening of Diwali. Wearing brand new saris donated to them by local organizations and holding diyas in their hands, they marched toward the *ghats* (steps) leading to River Yamuna. The surprised crowds cheered them on. The widows lit diyas and set them afloat on the river. The lighting of the diyas was doubly symbolic for them. They not only raised awareness about cleaning the polluted river, but they also warded off decades of darkness and isolation the widows endured after the death of their husbands.

The organizers reported that the "old girls" were excited and designed their own rangolis, sang songs from old films and played with sparklers with childlike delight.

Indian widows participate in Diwali.
Roberto Schmidt/AFP/Getty Images

Diwali in North America Now

Diwali is undergoing a metamorphosis in North America. It has been transforming in subtle ways. For immigrants who came in the 1960s and 1970s, Diwali was a simple event, a small affair that the mainstream didn't even know about. Friends gathered together to celebrate with homemade sweets and reminisce about Diwali in India. It was also celebrated on the closest weekend after the festival. No one ever thought of taking a so-called *faith day* off.

The family puja is still done at home, but people are now congregating in temples afterward to participate in communal prayers, conducted by priests. Some temples

The BAPS Swaminarayan Mandir, or temple, in Toronto is made of 24,000 pieces of hand-carved Italian marble and was constructed according to the guidelines given in ancient Hindu scriptures. Hundreds of artisans put the temple together using only chisels and hammers because the structure contains no nails or steel.

The BAPS Swaminarayan temple in Toronto, Canada.

are breaking traditions and are focusing less on the religious part and more on the celebrations, in the hope of attracting younger people to the services. Diwali **melas**, or fairs, are prevalent in cities across North America. A lot of event organizers have worked very hard over the past decades to make Diwali a mainstream festival.

Diwali came to Times Square for the first time in September 2013. Times Square, in the heart of New York City, is famous for its New Year celebrations. Each year, millions of people from all over the world watch the televised countdown of the final seconds of the year and celebrate the beginning of the New Year. After years of hard work, the South Asian event organizers brought the once invisible festival to the mainstream. Thousands of people attended the spectacular celebration. The all-day event featured musical performances, ethnic Indian dances, fashion shows, rangoli competitions, and sari draping workshops. Food from the

Rangoli.
Sanrb1974/Dreamstime.com

Indian subcontinent and appearances by Bollywood stars drew the biggest crowds.

The event concluded with a "Light Up Times Square" concert and a digital fireworks display. The organizers wanted to show the world how rich and diversified Indian culture is, and there couldn't be a better place to show that than Times Square, also known as the "Crossroads of the World." It was a historic moment for Indians, who felt they had finally "arrived" in the land they had immigrated to. That first Diwali at Times Square was so well attended that in 2014 the event became even bigger, and it will probably become an annual affair. Despite the religious connotations, Diwali has emerged as a secular event and the most representative festival of India.

Diwali Facts

Lord Ganesha, the elephant-headed god, shares the altar with Lakshmi on the night of Diwali. He always sits to her right. Although there are no Diwali legends associated with him, Hindus believe he must be kept happy at all times. Because he is India's favorite deity, he has a way of showing up at all Hindu festivals, and Diwali is no exception. He promises a year free from obstacles, and it's difficult to say no to that.

Ganesha.
Rakshashelare/iStock.com

Writers such as Rohinton Mistry, Shauna Singh Baldwin, Anita Rau Badami, Amitav Ghosh, Deepak Chopra and Jhumpa Lahiri, filmmakers Deepa Mehta, Mira Nair and M. Night Shyamalan, comedians Russell Peters and Aziz Ansari, actors Kal Penn and Mindy Kaling, and chef Vikram Vij have all helped Indians secure a place in North America's cultural history.

Today, immigrants from India are comfortably *assimilated* into Western culture. They wear Western clothes but also keep their traditions alive. Most of them consider themselves Canadian or American but at the same time maintain strong ties with India and feel a deep responsibility to preserve its culture. Music, literature, movies, art exhibitions and festivals are all ways to strengthen connections to ancient traditions.

For Indian people, no other occasion brings back memories like Diwali does. Many immigrants take their children to India so they can have an authentic experience of Diwali, and others recreate the celebrations for their children in their own homes. Children are taken to commercial Indian neighborhoods known as "Little Indias" to choose new outfits and buy mithai. Many parents fear that if this link with their culture is lost, their children will lose all ties to their heritage. And perhaps that's the reason they celebrate Diwali a bit more elaborately. They make temple visits and throw Diwali parties at home. In some places there are Diwali melas, replete with parades, floats, Bollywood dancing, buffets of Indian food, fireworks and of course mithai, lots and lots of mithai.

Author's daughter spelling out the word *Diwali* with a sparkler.

Amrita Singh

"The demographic mix is starting to change in Caledon. So it's important to celebrate all of the cultures that make up our student body."
—*Valerie Cunningham, Vice-Principal, Ellwood Memorial Public School, Caledon, Ontario*

The children of immigrants—the second generation—are often caught between two cultures. They may share the traditional values of their parents but also feel very comfortable in the Western setting. Most of them learn to balance the two cultures. It's easy for them to relate to North American culture because they are surrounded by it. But they have to work a little harder to make sense of their inherited culture, and they do that either by celebrating religious festivals like Diwali with their families and community or making frequent trips to India.

For the younger generation, Diwali has become a metaphor that defines who they are. With feet planted confidently in both cultures, young South Asians are creating a "fusion" Diwali. North America offers an amazing opportunity for people to experience a blend of cultures, languages and cuisines. As children, they enjoyed celebrating Diwali at home with their families. As adults, they are embracing traditions but modernizing them. They have no emotional attachment to the way Diwali is celebrated in India, but they want to teach their own children how to celebrate Diwali—their way—with dancing, food, sweets and fireworks minus the prayers. Diwali, for the younger generation, has evolved into a cultural festival.

Amritsari Kheer with Rose Water.
Rina Singh

Recipe by Vikram Vij

Amritsari Kheer with Rose Water

Ingredients:

10 to 12 green cardamom pods
(available at Indian supermarkets)

¾ cup basmati rice

12 cups full-fat milk

1 cup sugar

2 tbsps rose water

⅓ cup raw unsalted almonds
(peeled or unpeeled)

Rose petals for garnish

Makes 10 cups

Directions:

Lightly pound green cardamoms and peel off the pods. Empty brownish-black seeds into a medium pot. Discard the pods. Add rice and milk, and bring to a gentle boil on medium-low heat. Simmer, stirring gently and regularly, for about 1 hour and 10 minutes. Never scrape the bottom of the pot while stirring, otherwise you may get bits of slightly burned milk in your pudding. As the rice and milk cook, the consistency will become more and more like pudding. If the rice begins to clump or the milk begins to stick to the bottom of the pot, stir more often or turn down the heat slightly. (The milk burns quickly once it sticks and gives the entire pudding a burnt taste.) Remove the pot from the heat and add sugar. Add the rose water and stir well. To serve, divide rice pudding among individual bowls. Sprinkle almonds over the pudding just before serving. Garnish with rose petals.

Mitra's Story

Widows of Vrindavan.
Sulabh International Social Service Organisation

Mitra (not her real name) is seventy years old and has lived in Vrindavan for the last fifty years. She was born in Calcutta, more than 1,300 kilometers (800 miles) away. She lost her mother at a very early age and was barely twelve years old when her marriage was arranged to a sixteen-year-old boy. She remembers being happy on her wedding day because of the new clothes she got to wear and all the attention she got. Marriage also meant she would no longer have to go to school. She hated school.

Her husband's family was kind to her, but two years into the marriage, her husband died in a road accident. She became a widow at fourteen. What was more devastating to her was that her in-laws turned against her. They blamed her for their son's death. As was customary in the Bengali tradition, they shaved her head and forced her to dress in white, the color of mourning. Her two elder sisters disowned her for fear of assuming responsibility for a widowed sibling. She continued to live with her in-laws for a year, but the verbal abuse became too much for her to bear. A distant relative suggested she go to Vrindavan where young widows like her lived. She boarded the train to Vrindavan and has never left the town since.

She begged for a living, slept in temples or little roadside shacks, and grew old on the streets. It was only fifteen years ago that Sulabh International took her in and gave her shelter in an **ashram**, or religious commune. She threads flowers to make garlands for temple offerings and sings devotional songs in order to earn two simple vegetarian meals a day. In the evening, she loves to attend Bengali and Hindi language classes the organization offers. It's ironic that the classes are her favorite part of the day now.

Diwali is a faint memory. As a child, she celebrated Diwali with her family. As a widow, she was forbidden to take part in festivals. It took a lot of courage for her to get dressed in a new sari and walk with a diya in her hand on the streets. It felt strange and good at the same time when she floated the earthenware lamp on the river. "I didn't know what to pray for so I prayed for all my sisters in the ashram," she says.

Widows in Vrindavan celebrate Diwali.
Sulabh International Social Service Organisation

Sapna's Story

> "Without deep strong roots holding you, it's hard to grow branches that reach the sky."
> —*Sapna Alim, resident of Toronto*

Sapna Alim, a resident of Toronto, became aware of Diwali at a young age. Both her mother and grandmother are proud Hindus, and Diwali was the biggest holiday they observed. However, she didn't really embrace the true meaning of Diwali until she became an adult and began searching for some answers about her own identity. She remembers being fascinated with India and had a yearning for Indian traditions, which she didn't always understand. As the years passed, Diwali became more and more important to her. It was an opportunity to make amends, to start fresh and to celebrate the triumph of good over evil. It helped foster hope and love whenever she went through a dark phase in her life. Christmas has also been a big part of her life, especially when she married a Canadian of British descent. "Every coin has two sides and every heart has two halves," she says pondering her present situation. Together, Diwali and Christmas make her complete. She feels blessed to be able to celebrate the two cultures. The essence of both celebrations, she believes, is the same—love, gratitude and family.

Born and brought up in Canada, Sapna was not surrounded by Diwali except within her family. She had to go looking for it. "I was always captivated with Diwali, but now that I have a daughter, I feel a desire to learn about it inside and out," she says. She wants to teach her daughter,

Naaya, everything she didn't know when she was growing up. She wants to see the look of pride in Naaya's blue eyes as she identifies with her Indian heritage. Marrying a non-Indian and having a daughter has given Sapna a heightened sense of why she must keep the traditions alive in her own family. Sapna is determined to teach her daughter whatever she has learned from her mother and grandmother. She hopes that Naaya will develop her own roots and identity with confidence. The only regret Sapna has is that she never learned Hindi, which would have allowed her to feel the meaning of Diwali more with her heart and less with her head.

Coincidently, all of her personal milestones and memorable moments have happened around Diwali. "I have celebrated a business, a marriage proposal, a home purchase and now a baby girl born in November," she says with a sparkle in her eyes. Her husband, Damian, loves Indian culture and celebrates Diwali with great enthusiasm in their home.

Naaya, on her first Diwali.
Amrita Singh

Decorations for Deepawali in
Little India, Singapore.
Chrishowey/Dreamstime.com

FOUR

Diwali Around the World

Diwali in India

Diwali, India's biggest holiday, is celebrated with great enthusiasm all over India, in large cities and tiny villages.

Jaipur

Every region in India celebrates Diwali in its own special way, but there are a few cities that stand out. Jaipur, also known as the Pink City in Rajasthan, is one of them. The city of traders goes all out to tempt Lakshmi in its own style. She is, after all, the goddess of wealth. In a country with an acute electricity shortage, the merchants have

Statue of the Hindu goddess Lakshmi.
Amrita Singh

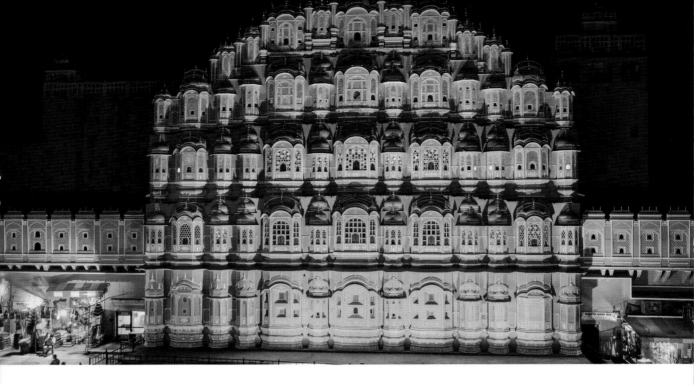

Hawa Mahal palace, Jaipur.
saiko3p/iStock.com

Local priests in Varansi perform the arti ceremony on the steps of the Ganges River for Diwali.
catshiles/iStock.com

a friendly competition for the brightest lit market. They turn on all the lights as they compete for the title of "Best Decorated Market." And they don't have to worry about the cost—the government foots the bill! The palaces and forts in this historic city are also beautifully lit with diyas and candles, making it a magical place on Diwali night.

Varanasi

Varanasi is the oldest continuously inhabited city on Earth, and it also happens to be the most sacred for Hindus. If Jaipur showcases the material side of Diwali, Varanasi offers visitors an unforgettable spiritual experience. There is no place like it on Earth—an open-air theater where people chant, bathe, have haircuts and cremate dead bodies. On Diwali, it has larger-than-life celebrations. Deities are paraded in chaotic streets, thousands of diyas placed in banana leaf bowls are floated on the Ganges River, and the priests perform the arti against the spectacular display of lights and fireworks.

West Bengal and Assam

While most Indians pray to Lakshmi, people in West Bengal and Assam worship Kali, the goddess of power and destruction. The legend goes that Kali came to Earth, killed all the demons, strung their skulls around her neck and lost control. She went on a rampage and destroyed everything in her path. Lord Shiva threw himself under her feet and she stopped in her tracks. Her eyes widened and she stuck out her tongue in shock as she realized that she was stepping on the god of destruction. She's lovingly known as Ma Durga, and her puja takes place before Diwali.

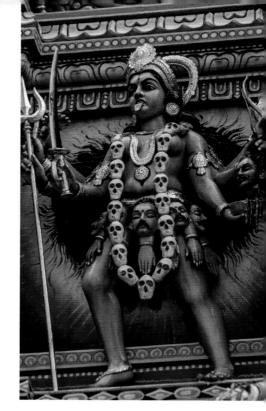

Statue of Kali.
Bridgendboy/iStock.com

Goa

In Goa, Diwali is also known as *Narakasura Chaturdashi*. It celebrates the destruction of Narakasura. On the eve of Diwali, giant effigies (crude representations) of the demon are stuffed with grass and firecrackers and paraded on streets. Businesses offer cash prizes for the scariest looking effigies. After the parades, just before sunset, the effigies are burned in open areas. This reminds people of the battle between Lord Krishna and the demon and how evil was destroyed. The next day, celebrations begin for Diwali. Diyas and candles are lit, as well as **akaash kandlis**, or sky lanterns,

> "For Hindus, Jains, Sikhs and Buddhists, lighting the lamp—the diya—is a chance to remember, even in the midst of darkness, that light will prevail."
> —*Barack Obama, President of the United States, in a video message on October 22, 2014*

67

Diwali Facts

The sari, perhaps the world's oldest unstitched garment, has survived centuries of fashion. The five and a half meters of fabric, ranging from hand-spun cotton to the finest of silks, is the ultimate canvas for weavers and designers to showcase their craft and style. Although the Western style of clothing is popular in urban India, 75 percent of the women in the country still wear saris. And of course they wear their best ones during the wedding season and at festivals like Diwali.

Dirty Wall Project.
Cindy Ryan, Director DWP

which can be seen hanging from roofs. Since Goa has a reputation for being a party city, and gambling is legal on Diwali night, people head to the casinos to try their luck.

Diwali in the Slums of Mumbai

When I was doing research for this book, I wanted to go beyond the lights, glitter, fireworks, sweets and gifts that are associated with Diwali. I began to wonder how poor children, especially the ones living in slums, celebrated Diwali, and if they also got excited. My research led me to a website called the Dirty Wall Project.

Kane Ryan, a young Canadian, founded the Dirty Wall Project. By the time he was twenty-seven, he had already worked his way around the world, arriving in India in 2009.

Dirty Wall Project.
Cindy Ryan, Director DWP

As he tells it, he was nervous about but fascinated by the enchanting chaos of the country. He spent many months traveling in trains and buses and was amused, saddened and baffled by the complexities of India. After a moving visit to an orphanage in the city of Chennai, Kane knew he would come back, but with a purpose. He wanted to make a difference in the lives of poor children. He returned to Canada and raised four thousand dollars and then went back to India and started the Dirty Wall Project. The name of the organization came from a series of photographs he took, exhibited and sold to raise money for the project.

In the last seven years, Kane, with the help of his parents, Cindy and Todd Ryan, have built a school in the Saki Naka slum community in Mumbai. The families

Dirty Wall Project.
Cindy Ryan, Director DWP

It's considered good luck to die in Varanasi, the holiest city of India. Hindu beliefs guarantee liberation from the cycle of rebirth. Instant nirvana!

living there receive financial support and medical assistance. Cindy and Todd Ryan now divide their time between Mumbai and Victoria.

In slums like Saki Naka, Diwali is celebrated with great excitement. It is very much a part of life for the children and their families. A few weeks before Diwali, the humble contents of homes are piled in laneways and the homes are swept, mopped and sometimes repainted. Before things are put back in the homes, they are washed and polished.

In the days leading up to Diwali, Cindy and the people working with the Dirty Wall Project gather the kids to paint clay diyas and make tissue paper *kandlis*. The girls love to draw **mehndi** (the traditional designs made with a paste of dried leaves of the henna plant) on each other.

They sit in crowded huts for hours playing Housie, a game similar to Bingo, with a chance to win a small prize. The kids decorate their school (a simple slum hut) with 3D works of art made with paper. Everyone prays to the goddess Lakshmi, and kids light firecrackers in laneways.

Like everywhere in India, each family has its own Diwali ritual, but everyone makes or buys sweets like ladoos and savory snacks like **chakli**. The kids wander the lanes handing out sweets. The community looks brighter during the Diwali season, and paper kandlis add to the festive look. Some families can afford to buy new outfits for kids, but others accept donated clothing. Children love to take pictures with Cindy's camera, and they excitedly wait for days to see the prints and get copies of their photographs.

Dirty Wall Project.
Cindy Ryan, Director DWP

Kids dressed in their best for their trip to the mall.
Cindy Ryan, Director DWP

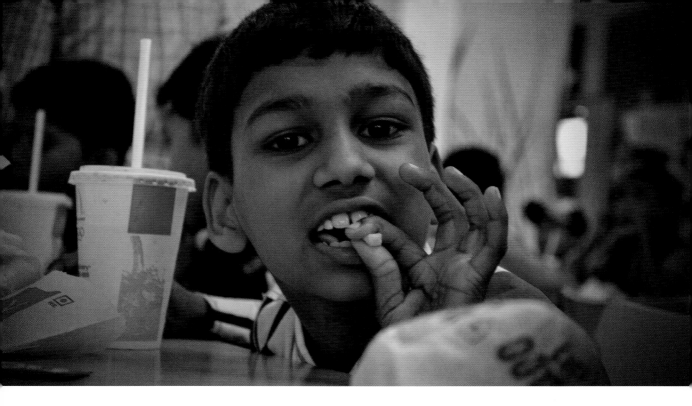

Tasting McDonald's for the first time.
Cindy Ryan, Director DWP

Kids painting diyas in the Saki Naka slums in Mumbai.
Cindy Ryan, Director DWP

The Dirty Wall Project organizes about three outings a year for kids. One of the outings is around Diwali. The kids prefer to call them picnics. Since they rarely get a chance to ride on public transport, the bus ride is quite an adventure, almost as exciting as the destination. They sing, play games and are generally very loud. They are so excited that they have to be kept from hanging out the windows of the bus.

In November 2014, during the Diwali season, the Dirty Wall Project rented a bus and took fifty-two kids to a fancy air-conditioned mall that had a giant bouncy castle, bumper cars and a McDonald's. The kids had dressed in their best clothes and combed or styled their hair. Safety pins held torn pockets and ruffles in place. Getting out of the community is a real treat for them because unless they attend school, the kids spend their days in the slum, playing with other kids, looking after younger siblings and doing household chores. Many of the kids are alone all day because their mothers work as caregivers for the children of middle-class and wealthy families.

During the trip, the kids didn't take anything for granted. The bus gave them a grand view of the city. The traffic, the buildings and the sea of people fascinated them. The play area, called Fun City, had the kids in fits of laughter. More fascinating than the bumper cars was the glass-walled elevator that delivered them to a magical world where the bathrooms had full-length mirrors, automatic soap dispensers and motion-activated faucets. The kids couldn't get enough of posing in front of the floor-to-ceiling mirrors, something they had never seen before. They were used to seeing only their faces in small mirrors hanging in their homes. It was hard to tear them away from their own reflections. They giggled as they waved their hands under soap dispensers and faucets to activate the sensors. They were amused by the neon-pink liquid soap. But it was the toilets that made them stand in awe. Used to public squat toilets, with no running water, they had no idea what to do with the fancy flushing toilets. Once they got the hang of it, they couldn't stop flushing, just to see the water disappear.

After the trip to the bathroom, the kids arrived at McDonald's, where fifty-two *McAloo Tikki* (potato patty) burgers were being prepared for them. Used to traditional Indian food made by their mothers, they looked suspiciously at the burgers. When a few brave kids took a first bite and gave the thumbs-up, others began to poke their fingers into the unfamiliar feast. A stranger came forward and pressed a thousand rupees into one of the organizer's hands to help pay for part of the outing.

Diwali Facts

South Indians continue to honor the ancient tradition of eating food served on a banana leaf. Especially popular during weddings and festivals like Diwali, a banana leaf is an environmentally friendly alternative to standard tableware. It's sturdy and large enough to hold an entire meal. Hygienic and chemical free, the leaf decomposes naturally, unlike plastic. The natural wax-like coating also lends its own flavor to the food, and the leaf can be folded in different ways to become a takeout container. It's very trendy to eat off of a banana leaf!

A South Indian banana leaf thaali.
yogesh_more/iStock.com

73

When the bus arrived back at the community, the kids were exhausted and happy to be home. The cost of the entire trip was 15,280 rupees. That's only $5.34 Canadian per child. For the kids, it was a priceless day.

Kerala

Kerala is the only state in India where Diwali is not celebrated. And like everything in India, there is a story behind it.

Long ago, Mahabali, a powerful king, ruled Kerala with great wisdom. The people of his kingdom prospered. Mahabali's popularity irked the gods, and they sent Vishnu, disguised as a poor little **Brahmin**, a person from the priestly class, to overthrow him. Vishnu begged for a

"May the Transcendent Light illumine your hearts, homes and communities, and may all your celebrations deepen the sense of belonging to one another in your families and neighborhoods."

—Cardinal Jean-Louis Tauran, in a message to Hindus in October 2014

Green tea plantations in Kerala.
Rina Singh

piece of land, just enough to take three steps. Mahabali, amused by the wish, granted it. No sooner had he agreed than Vishnu grew to gigantic proportions. His first step took over the entire land, his second covered the sky and he had nowhere to put his third step. Mahabali realized that Vishnu's third step would destroy the Earth so he offered his head. Pleased by the sacrifice, Vishnu allowed Mahabali one last wish. Mahabali wanted to come back once a year to visit his people and see them happy.

Onam, a two-week festival that takes place just before Diwali, is devoted to Mahabali. Since two major celebrations so close together would have been exhausting, the people of Kerala chose Onam over Diwali.

Getting a tilak in Kathmandu, Nepal.
Paul_Cooper/iStock.com

Mahabali would be proud of Kerala even today. It's the only state in India with a literacy rate of more than 93 percent, and all three communities (Hindus, Muslims and Christians) live in harmony.

Diwali Outside India

Diwali is celebrated wherever Indians live in the world. As the **diaspora** is growing, so is the number of countries in which the event is celebrated. While in some countries Indians celebrate it, in other places it has become a part of the local culture. In Japan, the city of Yokohama, which does not have a significant Indian population, goes all out to celebrate Diwali with Bollywood dances, traditional music and Indian food. People hang paper lanterns on trees.

Every year, around 200 to 300 people get injured in accidents in firecracker factories in Sivakasi, India.

Nepal

Nepal, once the only Hindu kingdom in the world, celebrates Diwali in a big way. Known as *Tihar*, it is celebrated with some variations. The festival honors Lakshmi and Ganesha and continues for five days. The first day is dedicated to the crow. The crow is a harbinger of death, and so by feeding it, the Nepalese believe they avoid any untimely deaths in the family.

The second day is *kukur tihar*, devoted to the dog. Even street dogs get a red tilak on their foreheads and can be seen wearing marigold garlands. They are well fed that day.

The third day is Lakshmi puja and the cow is worshipped too. The cow is given the status of a mother

Diwali Facts

Ramlila is a public dramatization of the epic story of Rama. It is performed during the festival of Dussehra by an all-male cast on make-shift stages across Northern India. Ramnagar, a town near Varanasi, hosts the grandest version.

Select scenes are enacted in different locations around town to hundreds of thousands of people. Rama and Sita's wedding draws the biggest crowd.

In 2005, UNESCO proclaimed the tradition of Ramlila, a masterpiece of the oral and intangible heritage of humanity.

Hindu temple in Little India, Singapore.
ronniechua/iStock.com

and therefore eating beef is illegal in Nepal. The fourth day is the beginning of the New Year. The houses are clean, the prayers to the gods and goddesses have been said, and so the people go into the streets to sing. This is called *bhailo.* The celebrations on the last day are similar to the traditions of India, where brothers and sisters renew their bonds with a tilak ceremony.

Great Britain

The biggest Diwali celebrations outside India are held in Great Britain, which has a large Indian population. The city of Leicester first made an attempt to celebrate Diwali in 1983. Belgrave Road is lined with Indian shops, and so the road was closed and the event was a huge success. Since then, Diwali celebrations have been getting bigger and bigger. Leicester Diwali is famous for its "switch-on" of lights, and about thirty thousand people gather to witness that as well as watch a display of fireworks and performances.

Diwali celebrations also take place at Trafalgar Square in London and have become an extravagant affair. People from all faiths attend the event.

Singapore

In Singapore, Diwali is known by its original name— *Deepavali.* The celebrations are held in Little India, a flourishing district. As in Britian, Singapore has a "switch-on" of lights to usher in Diwali. Fireworks are banned, but sparklers are allowed. Diwali is promoted as

a big tourist attraction, and therefore the religious part of the celebrations takes place in the temples. Little India offers a feast of Diwali foods, glittering lights and open-air concerts.

Banners to celebrate Deepavali in Little India, Singapore.
LeeYiuTung/iStock.com

Thailand

Thailand is mostly a Buddhist country but with strong Hindu roots. Ayutthaya, the former capital of Thailand, was named after Ayodhya, the birthplace of Lord Rama. Over centuries, Hinduism and Buddhism have fused so much that people don't even question some of the Brahmin rituals they follow. **Loi Krathong**, the festival of lights, is Thailand's version of Diwali. Elsewhere, Diwali is celebrated on the

Candles float in front of young Buddhist monks at a Loi Krathong ceremony at the Wat Pan Tao temple in Chiang Mai, Thailand.
Lazyllama/Dreamstime.com

Loi Krathong festival in Lampang, Thailand.
Ssenathee395/Dreamstime.com

darkest night of the month, but Loi Krathong is celebrated on a full-moon day of the twelfth lunar month, which falls most often in November. Banana leaves are cut and secured with toothpicks to make lotus-shaped bowls. Each bowl holds a small candle, a flower, a coin and a stick of incense, and the bowls are lowered into the Chao Phraya River as an offering to the river goddess. The floating away of diyas symbolizes letting go of anger. In the city of Chiang Mai, the festival is a major tourist attraction.

South Africa

Cape Town in South Africa has celebrated Diwali publicly since 2009. The event is colorful, noisy and vibrant. It includes Indian bazaars selling curries, fabrics and jewelry. There are stage productions with Bollywood dancing and

bhangra beats (dance music combining Punjabi folk traditions with Western pop music). People of all faiths are encouraged to attend. In fact, *The Witness*, a South African newspaper, published this entreaty one Diwali: *A call is made to all South Africans, whatever color, creed, race or religion, to light candles and lamps and display them in front of their homes on November 16 from 7 pm. This will show unity in diversity and your place in a rainbow nation.*

"At this time of Diwali and as I light this sacred lamp I am aware of how this lamp symbolizes the triumph of enlightenment over blind faith, prosperity over poverty, knowledge over ignorance, good health and well being over diseases and ill health, freedom over bondage."
—*Nelson Mandela, in an address at the Diwali celebration in Durban, South Africa, in 1991*

Suriname

Suriname is the smallest country in South America, and about 40 percent of its population is of Indian origin. The people are descendants of the nineteenth-century indentured workers. What is unique about Diwali in Suriname is that an annual procession takes place in the city of Paramaribo, and children and youngsters dress up as gods and goddesses. People clean their homes, share sweets and do Lakshmi puja. Dressed in their best clothes, they dance on the floats that are paraded in the streets.

Trinidad

Diwali came to Trinidad 170 years ago. In 1845, the British brought the first batch of indentured Indian workers to Trinidad. Slavery had been abolished a decade before (1834), and there was a shortage of workers in the sugar cane plantations. The British rounded up the poorest of the poor people from the Indian states of Bihar and Uttar Pradesh and sent them to Trinidad. The British

Bangles.
Rina Singh

In some Hindu temples, **annakut,** or "a mountain of food," is offered to the gods on Diwali. According to Guinness World Records, the largest annakut (an offering of 1,247 vegetarian dishes) was prepared in BAPS Swaminarayan Mandir in London, England.

plantation owners promised a minimum wage of 25 cents a day for men (16 cents for women), accommodation and basic health care. The contracts were for three to five years, after which the workers were free to find other work or remain for another term to earn a free passage back to India. Two hundred and nineteen Indians arrived on May 30, 1845, after enduring a long and difficult journey (many died en route). The hundred-day journey was the first test of courage for the *jahaji* (ship) brothers as they dropped their differences in social class and developed a deep bond that helped them survive the worst imaginable conditions that awaited them on the sugar island (or *chinya dweep* as they called it). Because Indians were perceived to be not physically as strong as black workers, they were flogged and subjected to starvation, disease and separation from family members. They were called *coolies.* Anyone found escaping the plantation was beaten to death to teach others a lesson.

Returning to India was not an option, because the young men and women had left without the permission and blessings of their parents. Trinidad became their home, and they held on to their traditions and recreated the religious festivals from memory. Diwali was one such festival that they cherished and continued to practice in their homes. Indians living in Trinidad, who had no contact with their motherland, remained emotionally attached to the country they left behind. They kept the stories of their gods, kings and demons alive by telling and retelling them. They crafted icons of their gods and goddesses out of clay and wood. For about 120 years, Diwali remained in the villages. As the Indian community evolved, so did their celebration. From their homes,

A girl lights a diya on the night of Diwali in Filicity, Trinidad.

Sean Drakes/LatinContent/ Getty Images

Divali Nagar has begun to be celebrated in countries around the world. These are dancers participating in a Divali Nagar festival in Queens, New York.
Buddy Singh (Digital Photo Buddy)

streets and more public spaces, and Divali Nagar (the City of Lights) was established.

Over the last fifty years, it has evolved from a rural and a spiritual celebration to a national and a cultural festival in contemporary Trinidad. Approximately two hundred and fifty thousand people come to Divali Nagar for the celebrations. Hindus wanted a greater recognition of their culture, and in 1966, Diwali was declared a public holiday. The Hindus kept the rituals of the evening prayers and lighting of diyas intact. But Diwali at the national level spiraled out of control. It became an opportunity to show-case Indian culture. Without any specific guidelines from the priests or any religious institution, Diwali celebrations embraced Bollywood dances, fashion shows, orchestras, and even a beauty pageant—*Miss Divali Nagar*.

One unique feature of Trinidadian Diwali is bamboo cannons. Green bamboo is not only bent artistically to display diyas, but cannons are also made out of it to make noises that resemble the sound of firecrackers. They were traditionally used for Christmas but were adopted for Diwali. Today, bamboo cannons are being slowly replaced with modern firecrackers. When businesses began to sponsor fireworks, Indians were excited that Diwali had become an important festival on their national calendar.

Cucumber Raita.
Rina Singh

Cucumber Raita

Ingredients:

1 ½ cups low-fat yogurt

½ English cucumber

1 tsp sugar

½ tsp chaat masala
(available in Indian grocery stores)

½ tsp dry roasted cumin powder
(cumin seeds are dry roasted
before grinding)

½ tsp paprika

½ tsp salt or to taste

Pinch paprika

Directions:

Stir yogurt in a bowl until smooth. Wash and grate cucumber with skin on. Combine all the ingredients together and refrigerate. Sprinkle a pinch of paprika to garnish. Serve cold. Try it with curries to cool the palate or as a dip for poppadoms.

Diwali lights.
Amrita Singh

Rangoli.
Dreamstime.com

A final word from the author

Writing this book has deepened the meaning of Diwali for me. As I researched the festival, I learned about some legends and rituals that I didn't know existed. I met sincere people who kindly shared their stories with me. To them I'm grateful. But what affected me most was my interview with Cindy Ryan, who runs the Dirty Wall Project in India. Diwali celebrates the victory of good over evil and light over darkness, but she and her family have truly turned their lives into a metaphor for light by bringing hope and joy into some disadvantaged lives.

Their story has inspired and humbled me, and I hope to celebrate future Diwalis not just by lighting my own home, but also by bringing light into the lives of those less fortunate than me.

A note from the series editor

"The Origins are built on the bedrock of personal stories, enhanced by careful research and illuminated by stunning photographs. No book can be all things to all people, and no two people experience a culture in the same way. The Origins are not meant to be the definitive word on any culture or belief; instead they will lead readers toward a place where differences are acknowledged and knowledge facilitates understanding."

—Sarah N. Harvey

Glossary

akaash kandlis—sky lanterns, often seen hanging from roofs during Diwali

amavasya—the darkest night of the month of Kartika, or the night of the new moon, and the night Diwali is celebrated on

annakut—"a mountain of food" offered to the gods on Diwali

arti—ceremony of worship

Ashoka chakra—a 24-spoke wheel, representing the teachings of Buddha

ashram—a religious commune

assimilation—the process by which one culture or language slowly changes or adapts to resemble another

asura—power-seeking deity (demon)

avatar—manifestation of a deity

bhangra—a folk dance from Punjab

Brahmin—priests, teachers and protectors of sacred learning

chakli—deep fried, spiral shaped, savory Indian snack

Dhanteras—the first day of Diwali

devas—gods

diaspora—a group of people living outside of the area in which their ancestors lived

Diwali—row of lights, from Sanskrit *deepa* meaning "light" and *vali* meaning "row"

diyas—oil lamps made of clay

Dussehra (*dasha-hara* in Sanskrit)—the day Rama defeated Ravana, the ten-headed demon, celebrated twenty days before Diwali

effigy—an image or crude figure representing a hated person

gurdwara—Sikh temple

Guru Granth Sahib—the Sikh holy book

gurus—spiritual teachers

indentured labor—a system of bonded labor similar to slavery

Kartika—a month in the Hindu calendar, which is based on the position of the sun and the moon

ladoos—ball-shaped sweets

langar—a free vegetarian meal offered to all regardless of faith or social class

Loi Krathong—the festival of lights, Thailand's version of Diwali

mantras—sacred chants

melas—fairs or festivals

mehndi—traditional designs made with a paste of dried leaves of the henna plant

mithai—Indian sweets, especially popular during Diwali

moksha—freedom from the cycle of rebirth; also called nirvana

nirvana—salvation from the cycle of life and death; also called *moksha*

prasad—devotional offerings that are shared among devotees

puja—prayer

racial slur—a name used to insult someone based on their race, ethnicity or nationality

rajah—prince

Ramlila—a theatrical rendition of Rama's life

rangoli—intricate designs on floors or in courtyards made with rice flour and colored sand or powder (also called *kolam* in South India)

Sanskrit—the primary sacred language of Hinduism

sari—a garment worn by South Asian women that is created from a single piece of fabric usually six yards long

swastika—a very old, sacred Hindu symbol for good fortune or well-being, from Sanskrit *su* meaning "well" and *asti* meaning "being"

thaalis—large platters

tilak—a mark worn on the forehead, made by mixing vermilion, water and rice; a symbol of the third eye of Lord Shiva

REFERENCES AND RESOURCES

Chapter One

Books:

Sekar, Radhika & Katherine E. Allen. *Festival of Light*. India: Vakils, Feffer & Simons, 2007.

Vij, Vikram & Meeru Dhalwala. *Vij's Elegant and Inspired Indian Cuisine*. Vancouver: Douglas & McIntyre, 2006.

Websites:

Diwali: The festival of lights. www.diwalifestival.org

Chapter Two

Books:

Kazimi, Ali. *Undesirables: White Canada and the* Komagata Maru—*An Illustrated History*. Vancouver: Douglas & McIntyre, 2012.

McDaniel, Jan. *Indian Immigration*. Broomall, PA: Mason Crest Publishers, 2004.

Makhijani, Pooja & Elena Gomez. *Mama's Saris*. New York: Little Brown, 2007.

Singh Jagpal, Sarjeet. *Becoming Canadians: Pioneer Sikhs in Their Own Words*. Madeira Park, BC: Harbour Publishing, 1994.

Websites:

BBC: What is the festival of Diwali? www.bbc.co.uk/newsround/15451833

Chapter Three

Books:

Daynes, Katie. *The Story of Diwali*. London, UK: Usborne Publishing, 2008.

Chapter Four

Books:

Heiligman, Deborah. *Celebrate Diwali with Sweets, Lights and Fireworks*. Washington, DC:
    National Geographic, 2008.

Websites:

National Geographic Kids: Diwali. www.kids.nationalgeographic.com/explore/diwali

Diwali Mela: Diwali Celebrations Around the World. www.diwalimela.com/aroundtheworld

Dirty Wall Project. www.dirtywallproject.com

INDEX

*Page numbers in **bold** indicate an image; there may also be text related to the same topic on that page*

Diwali lights.
Joat/Shutterstock.com

Acknowledgments

This book would not have been possible without the help of many people. Special thanks to Amrita Singh, M.S. Sodhi and Joginder Sharma for going out on Diwali and taking pictures in Toronto and in India.

Special thanks to Cindy Ryan, Swati Khurana, Sapna Alim, Aditya Rattan and Nimrat Randhawa for sharing their stories with me. Thanks to Shiva and Jennifer Mahadeo for teaching me about Diwali in Trinidad.

Thanks to Monique Polak, who read early drafts of this book, and Marilyn Pinchuk for reading the later ones.

And a very special thanks to Chef Vikram Vij, the Canadian culinary legend, for allowing me to use two of his festive recipes for this book and to Dheeraj Paul for letting me use his photograph of the Golden Temple.

Thanks also to the entire team at Orca Book Publishers, especially Rachel Page, the designer, and Sarah Harvey, my amazing editor, who spotted every mistake and asked all the right questions, pushing me to dig deeper into the story of Diwali.